Your Church Wedding

Mary Thompson

Jay books

Jay books
30 The Boundary, Langton Green, Tunbridge Wells, Kent TN3 0YB, England

First published 1989 by Tim Tiley Ltd
Second edition 1991 by Jay books

© Mary Thompson 1991

All rights reserved. No part of this publication may be reproduced or transmitted in any form or by any means, electronic or mechanical, including photocopying, recording, or any information storage and retrieval system, without permission in writing from the publishers.

This book is sold subject to the Standard Conditions of Sale of Net Books and may not be resold in the UK below the net price given by the publishers in their current price list.

ISBN: 1 870404 11 4

Typeset and printed in the European Community by
Gospel Communication, Tunbridge Wells.

This booklet is intended as a guide to planning a wedding in church. I hope it will be helpful to brides and bridegrooms and to their families. A wedding should be a joyful occasion, free from worry, and a marvellous start to a long, happy marriage.

As the wife of a clergyman, I am frequently a wedding guest. I have had the opportunity to meet and talk with many wedding couples and their parents. I have shared in the excitement—and sometimes in the anxieties—of wedding planning. I am aware of points that can cause worry, disputes and tension, and I have noticed the extra touches that please the couple and their guests.

This booklet is based on what I have learned from sharing in plans, observing couples preparing for a wedding, and then being a guest on their great day. Every wedding is a unique occasion with its individual atmosphere. Each couple make their own decisions about the way they want their wedding organised and celebrated. This booklet simply offers information and ideas to help couples plan the style of church wedding that they, their families and guests will enjoy and remember with pleasure.

I am very grateful to all the couples who have invited my husband and me to their wedding. Many of them have become our friends. I hope the experience they have so willingly shared will be useful to all who read this booklet.

Preparations

The decision to marry is reached: engagement rings are bought, announcements appear, congratulations and presents arrive, often an engagement party or family celebration is held. Being engaged is an exciting stage to enjoy for itself for a few weeks, months, or even years. Make the most of the time before you become immersed in wedding plans.

Where to marry

A basic decision for those in England and Wales is whether to be married in church or registry office. In Scotland couples can also be married in hotels, reception rooms and private houses. If proposals presented to Parliament, for reform of the system for registering marriages in England and Wales, are accepted, couples in England and Wales will also have this freedom.

Marriage in the Church of England or the Church in Wales

A person over the age of 16 is entitled to be married in the church of the parish where he or she lives or has a parental home, or is a member of the Electoral Roll. Without the residential qualifications or membership of the

Electoral Roll, a person does not have a right to be married at a church which is not their parish church. To be married in their parish church it is not necessary for either of the couple to be baptised or regular church-goers.

Electoral Roll

Before his or her name can be entered on the Electoral Roll of a church, a person must regularly attend worship in that church for at least six months. Either a bride or groom can qualify to be married at any Church of England or Church in Wales church by being on the Electoral Roll of that church.

Marriage without residential qualifications

Sometimes a couple wish to be married in a church for which they do not have residential or Electoral Roll qualifications. This may be because:

> one or both of the couple attend the church regularly,
> the church has some special significance for the couple, eg a link with one of the Forces in which a member of the family has served,
> one of the couple belongs to a Guild or organisation associated with the church,
> there is an attachment to a school or college attended by one of the couple,
> there is a long-standing family connection,
> it is near where one of the couple works,
> they have special regard for the church's architecture, music or clergy,
> it has ease of access for guests and /or proximity to the place where the wedding reception will be held.

Legal requirements

Marriage can take place in a Church of England or Church in Wales church after any of the following requirements have been fulfilled:

> Banns have been called and certificates have been issued to say that these have been duly called.
> A Common Licence has been obtained.
> An Archbishop's Licence has been obtained.
> A Superintendent Registrar's Certificate has been obtained.

Marriage by Banns

When a couple have residential or Electoral Roll qualifications for marrying in a church, marriage is usually by banns. The banns naming the couple must be read at public worship in the church of the parish where each person is resident, or on the Electoral Roll, on three Sundays before the wedding. The marriage must take place within three months of the final calling of the banns.

House, Edinburgh, or local registration offices in Scotland, sets out the legal procedure for marriage in Scotland.

If you want to be married in a Scottish church of any denomination, go and see the minister or parish priest who will give you a church form to complete. This form is in addition to the marriage notice that must be submitted to the registrar of the district where the marriage is to take place at least 15 days before the date of the proposed marriage. (It is wise to allow at least four to six weeks.) If the registrar is satisfied that there is no legal impediment to the marriage, he will issue the prospective bride or bridegroom with a Marriage Schedule, specifying the date and place of marriage. This schedule must be produced to the approved person who is to conduct the religious marriage.

The Episcopal Church of Scotland

Where one or both partners are baptised and have some link with that church, or another church within the Anglican communion, and neither party has a previous partner still living, marriage can take place in a Scottish Episcopal Church.

If there is a previous partner still living, a Certificate of Authorisation, allowing a Scottish Episcopal Church wedding, may be granted by the diocesan Bishop. To apply for such a certificate, consult the parish priest, who will sign your application form, pass it on to the Bishop and be interviewed by the Bishop with you. You should allow at least three months for this procedure; a firm date for the wedding should not be arranged until the authorisation is granted.

If a couple cannot be married in a Scottish Episcopal Church, it is possible to have a service of blessing after a registry office ceremony. The form the blessing service will take is usually planned by the clergy in discussion with the couple.

The Church of Scotland

To arrange a marriage in a Church of Scotland church, consult the minister of the local church or the Church of Scotland church you wish to use. He or she will inform you about the banns and the legal requirements. At the discretion of the minister, marriage in a Church of Scotland church is possible for those who have been divorced and have a previous partner still living. Each couple's situation is considered individually.

Marriage in the Church of Ireland

In this church, wedding arrangements are made with the incumbent or Rector of the parish — much as in England. There is marriage by banns for baptised members of the church who have been resident in the parish for at least three months.

Those who are not church members can obtain an Ordinary Licence from a Registrar and be married in the church of the parish where one or both partners are resident.

Anyone who wishes to marry in the church of a parish where neither of the couple reside must be an 'accustomed member' for at least three months before the wedding or obtain a Special Licence from the Bishop of the diocese. For this licence, there is a fee of up to £50. It is also possible to be married in a building (such as Trinity College Chapel, Dublin) which is not licensed for weddings, but for this an Archbishop's Licence must be obtained.

Those who have been divorced from a partner still living cannot be married in a Church of Ireland church, but at the Rector and Bishop's discretion they may be given a service of blessing.

For information on the legal arrangements for marriage in Northern Ireland contact the Registrar's Office, City Hall, Belfast, and ask for a Guide Paper to Marriage in Northern Ireland. For information on marriage in the Republic of Ireland, write to General Register Office (Oifig an Ard-Chláraitheora), Joyce House, 8/11 Lombard Street East, Dublin 2, and ask for the information sheet, Marriage in the Republic of Ireland.

Legal requirements

For marriage in English or Welsh churches, other than the Church of England or the Church in Wales, it is necessary for one or both of the couple to live in the Registration District in which the church is located. Notice must be given to the local registrar who will issue a form for the couple to complete. This is exhibited in the Town Hall not less than three weeks and not more than three months before the marriage date, and the couple are then issued with a certificate of authority for marriage (equivalent to a Banns Certificate) which must be given to the authorised person conducting the marriage. In a Catholic church a notice about the wedding is usually displayed in the church as well as in the Town Hall.

In all these churches arrangements for flowers, organ and choir are made in much the same way as this booklet suggests for Anglican churches. Plans should be discussed with the minister or priest.

Fixing the date

When you have decided on a church where you would like to be married, choose some possible dates. If you know where you want the reception held, discover which dates are still available there. Do not make any firm arrangements until you have seen the priest or minister and fixed the date and time of the wedding. Sometimes a bride will book hall and caterers and then find to her dismay that the church already has a wedding booked for the date and time she wanted. Booking the date and time of the wedding service should be the priority.

Church notice boards and magazines usually advertise a telephone number for obtaining information or the time at which the priest or

minister is available to see wedding couples. You could call then, telephone, or speak to the priest or minister after a service to arrange a mutually convenient time to discuss the wedding.

If you are not familiar with the church you have in mind for the wedding, you could attend a Sunday service and discover the feel of the church, before asking if it would be possible to be married there. The bride's family may also like to attend a service at the church before finalising plans.

Who conducts the wedding?

In the Church of England or Church in Wales, the priest will agree that he or one of his curates will marry you in the church, and the date will be booked. In the Church of England, woman deacons are legally able to conduct weddings, and many couples are happy for a woman deacon to conduct or take part in their church wedding, but if you have strong feelings about a woman taking the service it is wise to discuss these at an early stage.

In a Baptist, Methodist or United Reformed Church, the marriage will be conducted by the man or woman authorised for that church. In a Catholic church it will be conducted by the parish priest or one of his staff.

Clergy of most churches are authorised to conduct religious marriages, and in the Methodist, United Reformed and Baptist churches lay or ordained persons are appointed by the local registrar as an 'authorised person' to conduct marriages in a particular church. Roman Catholic priests are appointed as authorised persons for their churches. If the person conducting the marriage is not a registrar, or authorised for that church, it is necessary for a registrar to attend the ceremony.

If you want a clergy friend or relation to marry you or to take part in the ceremony, you should discuss this with the person conducting the service. Most will happily agree. If one of the couple belongs to the Roman Catholic or a Free Church, it may be possible to invite the priest or minister to take some of the prayers or give the address at an Anglican wedding.

Planning

As there are many aspects of a wedding service that need discussion and planning, it is a good idea to fix future dates for interviews and rehearsals. On your second visit, take a list of points to check and discuss. These will include: number of people the church holds, form of service, service sheets, hymns, choir, organist, flowers, car parking facilities, whether there is a loo, confetti regulations, bells, availability of heating, permission to photograph, record or video in church. If you are thinking of holding the wedding reception in a Methodist or Baptist hall, and you want to serve alcohol, check whether it is allowed on the premises.

If you are being married by banns, ask the date and time of the three services at which they will be called. Most couples—and sometime parents too—like to be present for at least one calling of the banns. Hearing them is part of your wedding preparation. It is essential to collect the Banns Certificate from the church where you are not being married as you must give this to the clergyman at the church where the wedding will take place. There is generally a fee of £5 for calling each set of banns and a fee of £2.50 for the Banns Certificate.

Marriage preparation

As well as explaining the formalities, the priest or minister will probably tell you about marriage preparation groups, or ask you to come for marriage preparation interviews. He or she may also give you or suggest some books you could usefully read, or videos you could watch. Most clergy have considerable experience of preparing couples for marriage so it is worth taking advantage of any group or individual preparation you are offered.

At marriage preparation, you will be encouraged to think about the commitment you will be making and the factors that create a loving, stable and lasting marriage. Occasionally, after they have thoroughly thought and talked about what marriage means, couples change their minds and decide not to be married for a while or even not at all!

Fees

The Church of England has a statutory scale of fees for legal aspects of weddings, and church councils make their own scale of charges for extras, such as music, bells, additional heating and the verger's fee. The parish priest should show you a copy of the scale of charges and explain the fees to you. In the Church of England the basic marriage service fee is £39 and sometimes there is an additional parish clerk's fee of £10; the marriage certificate costs £2. The clergyman's half of the marriage service fee (£19.50) is not an 'extra' for him. However many marriages he conducts, the fees he receives are deducted from the salary paid to him by the Church Commissioners. The church's half of the fee (£19.50) is a very small contribution to the church's continuing running costs. All the wedding fees should be paid before the wedding. Other Anglican churches make their own fee arrangements which the clergy will discuss with you.

In the Baptist, Methodist and United Reformed churches, fees are generally minimal for church members; other couples are charged a reasonable fee to cover organ, flowers, heating and certificate costs. In the Catholic church there is no set scale of fees; the charges vary from church to church and are negotiated with the parish priest.

Reception plans

Even before you fix the day and time of your wedding service, you will probably have discussed what kind of reception you want to give, where to hold it, who will pay, and how much should be spent. Sometimes parents of the bride will meet the whole cost, some couples pay part and their parents pay the rest; at other times the couple share the cost between them. Each couple and their family make their own decisions about this. When discussing the reception, be sensitive to parents' views and try to meet at least some of their wishes — especially if they are going to pay. But, ultimately, it is important for the bride and groom to plan the kind of reception that they want to give.

Some couples choose a simple reception, so as to invite large numbers of guests; some want a more elaborate occasion — even though numbers may be limited by cost or the size of the home or reception venue; yet others compromise with a meal for close family and friends, followed by an evening disco/dance for contemporaries. Hopefully, all will come to a common mind, but it usually depends on how much everyone is prepared to spend and how they want to spend the money. It is essential to book the reception in good time, and it pays to get plenty of quotations.

Invitations

The invitations can be bought or printed as the couple wish. You may need to enclose a map, directions for reaching the church and reception venue, and information on parking. Keep a careful guest list and enter acceptances/refusals straightaway. Who to invite and who could be left out is always a bit of a headache. Bridegrooms' parents feel sad if they are allowed to invite only a few of their family and friends, while there are huge numbers of guests from the bride's family. Each couple has to try and resolve this amicably with their parents. Try not to leave out anyone who will be disappointed at not receiving an invitation. Whatever party or event people attend subsequently, nothing quite makes up for missing the wedding.

Your supporters

Attendants

Think carefully when choosing child attendants. Avoid any who are likely to show off, be awkward, or over-nervous. I think that under-threes tend to be rather overwhelmed and too young, but the child's parents should be able to tell you how a child is likely to behave. Help the child feel it is a privilege to be invited to attend you, and that you really want them to be there. A well chosen outfit and attractive hairstyle, plus the pleasure of the occasion, make any child look attractive, so don't rule out the plain or the plump. Consult the parents, then invite the child so that he or she feels that being an attendant is something he has chosen, not a duty that has been inflicted. See that the child attendants are taken to a wedding — or at least to see a bridal party outside a church — before your wedding; then they will have some idea of what to expect.

Gaining the child's co-operation over the clothes they are going to wear is vital. My daughter once thought she had a 'horrible' bridesmaid's frock; it was stiff taffeta and not at all the style she would ever have chosen. The bride bought it without consulting her. However, for another wedding she went with the bride to choose the pattern and fabric, and the dress was a great success. If you plan to dress child and adult bridesmaids in the same fabric or style of dress, beware of giving adult bridesmaids a 'little girl' look. It is an advantage if a child's dress will be suitable for subsequent parties, but that is not the first consideration. Make sure that all the outfits — bride's and attendants' — harmonise in colour and style and give a total effect looking related rather than just individually attractive. To ensure that a dress fits a child well, you may need to have it made — rather than bought ready-made. Avoid fiddly buttons, scratchy ruffs and collars, and any detail that is going to irritate or worry a child. An attendant who feels comfortable is more likely to behave well.

A friend told me that when she was a child she watched a 'pageboy' in a white satin suit come out of the house opposite; unnoticed by the rest of the bridal party he took off his white satin pumps and put them down a drain. 'I am not wearing these shoes', was evidently his message as, without anyone else noticing, he climbed into the car with just white socks on his feet.

The likely weather, cost, bride's and child's preferences, and the style of the church — especially whether it is light or dark, warm or chilly — will influence choice of outfits. Sometimes the child's parents offer to help with the cost — especially if the outfit will be useful in the future. If you want the child's hair styled by a hairdresser, ask the parents to organise an appointment — unless you have booked a hairdresser to come to the bride's house to do hair and arrange head-dresses on the morning of the wedding. Make sure head-dresses can be fastened securely so that there is no worry about them slipping askew.

Ushers

The couple will choose friends and relations to be ushers. Tell them the style of dress expected — morning or lounge suits — when you invite them. You want ushers who will welcome guests with a smile, give out the service paper graciously and escort the guests to their seats. Dignified, helpful ushers make quite a difference to guests who sometimes arrive flustered by travel delays. Many churches do not have a loo, so ushers should be able to tell guests where to find the nearest one. They should also be able to give advice about parking. For a large wedding, the ushers should be given a seating plan so that relations and close friends are shown to appropriate seats.

Best man

The bridegroom chooses a friend or relation to be his best and right hand man at the wedding. The best man should wear the same type of suit as the groom, so the groom and best man will need to discuss what kind of suits to wear. The bride can tell her father what they have decided.

A best man should be utterly reliable, punctual, and able to be businesslike about paying (with money given to him by the groom) drivers, delivery people and unpaid church, choir or verger fees. The best man is responsible for ensuring that all the guests can get from the church to the reception comfortably. He must also be able to make an audible and humorous speech at the reception — without being too anecdotal or lengthy — and it is his task to read any telemessages or greetings sent by absent friends and relations.

The best man accompanies the groom to the church, keeps the rings safely until he hands them to the officiant, and is generally reassuring to the groom. He will be expected to attend at least one rehearsal. It helps if he too pays a preliminary visit to the church, if possible for a service, so that the surroundings feel familiar when he appears at the wedding. At the reception he will join the parents and couple as they greet the guests. He will look after the bridesmaids, and help ensure that everyone is at ease and enjoying the reception.

If the groom changes out of hired clothes before going away, the best man generally takes responsibility for keeping these safely and for returning them. If the groom changes out of clothes he does not want to take on his honeymoon, the best man should check that someone is taking them home for him.

The bride's dress

There are plenty of illustrated magazine articles and catalogues, as well as shop displays of dresses, patterns and materials to help the bride choose her dress. Whether she makes it herself, allows a friend to make it, goes to a designer or dressmaker, or buys ready-made, is her choice. The bride's ideas, her size, and current fashions may change, so it is generally considered wise not to buy the dress too far in advance. A wedding dress hanging in a wardrobe for months before the wedding day can gather dust or even lose its allure. I think it is more exciting to buy the dress or have it finished quite near the wedding day when preparations are intensifying.

There is no need to choose a very expensive creation; the important thing is for the bride to feel absolutely confident about her dress. I have noticed how even brides who are not specially pretty do look radiant and lovely if they are happy on their wedding day.

Give plenty of time to choosing the dress, and never allow yourself to be hassled into buying if you have tried on several and none seem right on you however lovely the dresses may be. A wedding day should make everyone say: "The bride looks beautiful", rather than: "What a beautiful dress". Before buying a dress or fabric for making one, think about the amount of light in the church and how you will appear in the dress in artificial light as well as in daylight.

The back of the dress is important because this is what guests will see as you walk up the aisle and stand for the ceremony. Think carefully before choosing lacey, very fragile fabrics or an heirloom dress that may easily tear if accidentally stepped on. Have some regard for likely weather too. Even a highly glamorous dress loses impact when the bride's teeth chatter.

Choose shoes with care. Look for an elegant pair that will be comfortable and make walking easy. It is a pity to risk catching a heel in a grating or wobbling up steps because heels are too high or spikey. Also think about the height of the groom when choosing your shoes. I know one bridegroom who has never forgotten that on their wedding day, for the only time in her life, his wife looked taller than he did: she had borrowed some gold brocade very high heeled shoes! Remember to take price tickets off the soles or heels.

Some brides prefer to hire or borrow a dress, rather than to spend a large amount of money on a purchase unlikely to be worn again. People think they will wear their wedding dress subsequently for balls and parties, but in practice this does not seem to happen. The dress and what she spends on it is the bride's own decision. As a beginning, you will probably like to look at some wedding gowns on your own, though you may want your mother, a friend, or an adult bridesmaid to accompany you when you buy.

The Wedding Service

Form of service

In the Church of England most couples are usually given a choice between the 1662 Book of Common Prayer service and the modern Alternative Service Book service. Before deciding which form of service to choose, it is as well to go away and read over both. If you are not given a choice and dislike the form of service offered, ask to have the other form.

If you are a regular churchgoer, you may want to have the Marriage Service with Holy Communion. This form of service seems especially appropriate if at least some of your friends and relations are church members familiar with the Holy Communion Service.

With either the Prayer Book or Alternative Service Book form of service, the bride can decide whether or not to promise 'to obey' her husband.

In the Church in Wales, the Book of Common Prayer for use in the Church of Wales Holy Matrimony is the usual form of service. This appears in a bi-lingual form with facing Welsh and English pages, and the couple and priest together decide which language to use for the service. Another option in Wales is the 1662 Book of Common Prayer service, but this is seldom chosen.

In the Scottish Episcopal Church couples are likely to have a choice between the form of service in the Scottish Book of Common Prayer 1929 and the form in the The Alternative Service Book 1980 that is used in the Church of England.

The Roman Catholic Church has a basic marriage service with a variety of prayers, readings and blessings which the couple and parish priest can choose together. When the couple want a Nuptial Mass, this possibility should be discussed with the parish priest.

In a Methodist church, the Marriage Service from the Methodist Service Book is used, but couples are usually given some choice about prayers and readings. United Reformed and Baptist ministers tend to draw up a form of wedding service based on traditional wording, but couples are usually given some choices.

Hymns

Take trouble over choosing hymns. If you do not have a hymn book at home, ask to borrow one from the church so as to look at plenty of possibilities. You may think that 'The King of Love,' 'Jerusalem,' 'The Lord's my Shepherd' and 'Praise my soul the King of Heaven' are rather hackneyed, but wedding congregations always seem to like these, and if you want the congregation to sing you need well-known hymns. Some couples have chosen 'Dear Lord and Father of Mankind, forgive our foolish ways' or 'Fight the Good Fight', but when you think about the words they do not seem the most appropriate for the occasion.

Sermon

Some priests and ministers expect to give a short address, others give you the option. I think there is much to be said for having a sermon. It need not be long, but it helps to make the service personal to the couple and, hopefully, it will provide a thought or idea to remember. Your guests have come to take part in a service, you have invested much time, thought and money in making it the kind of ceremony you want, so why not include a sermon to help make it a more memorable occasion that touches guests as well as the couple. I am often surprised how much guests comment on the sermon.

Music

It is worth considering paying for a choir to lead the hymns and responses and sing an anthem while the registers are being signed. A choir can also sing 'God be in my Head', or some similar prayer, after the blessing. Feeble singing by wedding guests unaccustomed to singing hymns in church can be uninspiring.

Ask if the church has a choir and how much it costs for them to sing at a wedding, and ask about other choirs that sing in that church. As soon as you decide on a choir, make a firm booking. Remember, if you plan to

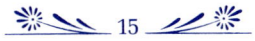

record or video the wedding service, you will have to pay a considerably higher fee to the choir, organist and perhaps the church. The Royal School of Church Music has a recommended scale of charges for the Church of England and Church in Wales.

It is usual to ask the regular church organist, who may also be the choirmaster, to play at a wedding. If you do not use the church choir and organist, but bring in another organist, you will be expected to pay the church organist a fee as weddings provide part of his or her salary. Be cautious about allowing a friend to play the organ for you unless you know that they are sufficiently experienced to play the music of your choice on an unfamiliar organ. In any case, your organist should arrange to practise on the church organ. A poor organist will be distracting.

Arrange to meet the organist and choirmaster to discuss the music for every part of the ceremony. Include the period during which the guests are arriving, as well as the time after the ceremony when they will be leaving. Gentle organ music can help set the atmosphere as guests arrive, and a joyful tune will send them out of the church with smiles. Tell the organist clearly what time you would like him to start playing. I have known professional organists who give poor value and dash into church only seconds before the bride.

If you want a guitar, violin or harp played, or a solo sung, discuss this with the organist and clergy at an early stage. Beware of making the wedding too much like a concert. At one recent wedding, I thought that choir anthems, plus two long violin pieces and a poem read by the bridegroom's mother, seemed rather excessive.

Service sheets

You can have service sheets printed or photocopied, or rely on prayer book or service booklet and hymn book. Sheets make it easier for the guests to follow the service. Ask the priest or minister to show you examples of service sheets from previous weddings. If you go to a printer, order in good time so that you can see proofs. It is essential to check proofs. If the bridegroom spells his name Antony, it is a pity for it to appear as Anthony on his wedding service paper. If you are producing your own service sheets you could incorporate a line drawing to give a personal touch. Make clear arrangements for collection or delivery of printed service sheets and for getting them to the church in good time on the day.

Confetti

Some churches ban confetti, or charge extra if it is thrown, as it makes a mess and takes time to clear away. If your church has such a stipulation, ask your guests to save their confetti for the reception.

Flowers

The flowers in church help to create atmosphere, as well as adding beauty to the building. Discuss choice of flowers with whoever is normally responsible for the church flowers. Some churches offer to buy the flowers and provide arrangements for an agreed fee. Many brides gladly accept such an offer, other brides prefer to be responsible for their own flowers. However, even if you do not wish the church flower arrangers to do the flowers for you, it is wise to listen to their advice. You will want to find out what vases they have available and the best positions for them before you buy the flowers.

In most churches, a few beautiful, large arrangements make more impact than scattered small vases. You would be wise to include tall single and/or spray chrysanthemums, carnations, pinks or lilies in your purchases. Though they look lovely, stocks, delphiniums and roses do not last as well. White, cream and yellow flowers show up well in a dark church. Make sure you buy or gather enough greenery.

Think carefully before you ask Aunt Sybil who is 'so good at doing flowers' to arrange the church flowers for you. You need either a professional or a skilled amateur who is accustomed to arranging flowers in a large building, not just in a home.

A glorious flower arrangement near the door gives a welcoming touch; other displays are usually placed near the steps where the couple will stand, on or near the altar, and in the area where the registers will be signed.

Some people like pew ends (made from flowers, greenery and ribbon inserted in oasis) fastened to the front pews or even to all the pews. After the ceremony these pew ends are sometimes given to guests. Some brides like an archway of flowers where they enter the aisle—but these can look overdone.

Should there be another wedding at the church on the same day as yours, you could meet the other couple and work out a scheme for flowers to please you all at a shared cost. If you plan to engage professional florists to do the flowers for you, ask to see photographs of their work at previous weddings, or, better still, go and see the flowers they have arranged for another wedding before you book them.

If you are buying the flowers yourself, use a florist or stall you know. Alternatively, ask the church flower arrangers where they buy the church flowers, or ask advice from someone who is keen on flower arranging. Before you set out to buy, work out approximately how many flowers you want and the amount you are prepared to spend on them.

When you go to a wholesale market you will not buy as cheaply as the traders and florists, but you should get more flowers for your money than you will in a shop. Notice which stalls the professional florists are using and what they are buying. Should the bride be allergic to flowers, buy some silk flowers in a store or wholesale market.

Photographs and videos

One wedding couple said to me: "What advice do you have to offer us, Mrs Thompson?" I think they expected some hints on marriage, but I said, "Do make sure you have a really, good professional photographer." When I think how much some people spend on weddings, I am amazed that they rely on amateurs to capture the day on film for them. Your wedding photographs are a record you are likely to keep for the rest of your lives. Looking at them should be a continuing pleasure, not an experience that leaves you wishing you had engaged a better photographer. Taking photographs at weddings is specialised. Professionals know where to position themselves, when to take pictures, and how to control guests. They usually take plenty of pictures so that the couple, family and friends have a wide choice. Encourage friends and relations to snap away, but also engage a professional who will do justice to the occasion. Black and white pictures last well; in a subtle way they capture the atmosphere of a wedding and encapsulate precious moments, so I strongly recommend having some black and white as well as colour photographs.

Some clergy do not allow photographs to be taken in church, as photography can be distracting during the ceremony. Find out the usual practice at your church and tell your photographer to be discreet. A bustling, pushy photographer can intrude on a wedding service. One couple I know felt they did not want any distractions during the actual ceremony so they confined their photographer to the porch. Other brides have been so conscious of the cameras they have almost given the impression they were acting in a film of a wedding rather than actually being married.

If you want a video made, you must obtain permission from the officiant beforehand. Some will agree to one being made in church. Others are not in favour as they think it can be disconcerting for the couple and make the wedding seem like a performance instead of a sacred and precious occasion. To have a video made, you must also obtain agreement from the organist, choir and any soloists, and pay them increased fees. One Vicar told me: "It is difficult when someone comes to take a video as a 'surprise' for the couple: they do not always realise the extra expense that will be involved."

However, a video does give an opportunity to watch your wedding again and again, and it is a reminder of how you made promises to each other. It also becomes a precious record of departed relations and friends dressed in their best and enjoying the occasion, so there is much to be said for it. Having a video made is becoming more usual, so obtaining agreement for it should not be too difficult — provided you ask beforehand.

Before the wedding, think out any special groups you want to have photographed, eg grandparents, colleagues with the bride, family groups. Give the photographer a list. You will probably want to include one picture with the officiant. It is also good to have one or two pictures of the flowers so that you have a lasting record of them.

Reception

There are plenty of books giving guidance on style and organisation of wedding receptions. This booklet is primarily concerned with making the most of the church wedding service, but the careful planning and thought put into the service is also needed for the reception if the occasion is to be enjoyed and happily remembered by everyone present.

One of the difficulties of a wedding reception is that often at least half the people sharing in the occasion do not know the rest of the people present, and they may never see them again after the reception is over.

Plan seating carefully. You can allot people to particular tables even if the food is served from a buffet. Ask a few friends and relations to introduce guests to each other and look after any who seem alone. Aim for a relaxed, friendly atmosphere where guests will feel free to introduce themselves to others and chat to anyone standing or sitting near to them.

By receiving guests as they arrive, you will, at least, greet each person, but it will be appreciated if you circulate after the meal and exchange a few words with each guest. I have been to only one wedding where I didn't have a chance to speak to the bride. She was determined not to be 'traditional', so dispensed with the usual receiving line. I think this was a mistake as other guests present who had travelled a long way also had no chance to speak to her.

Grace and thanks

A wedding reception invitation will be appreciated by the person who conducts your wedding. If he or she is married, include their partner. Generally, the clergy are happy to say grace, even if they have not been asked to do this beforehand, but if they are given prior notice they can think out especially appropriate wording. If you should want the officiant to make a speech, do not spring it on him; ask him in advance.

In their speeches, the bridegroom or the bride's father could include a few words thanking the clergy for the trouble taken over arranging and conducting the service. If the choir have been invited to the reception, they could also be thanked.

After the wedding is over

If you write and thank or send postcards to people, such as flower arrangers and soloists, who have played a special part in your wedding, that will please them. Sometimes, after a wedding that has taken a great deal of time and work to arrange, a couple wave goodbye, set off on their honeymoon and are never seen by the church again. However, most couples like to keep in touch as they feel that the church where they were married is significant to them. They come at Christmas, Easter and near their wedding anniversary, if not more regularly. Some couples ask to have their babies baptised in the church.

Some of the tasks involved when planning a church wedding

You may not wish to carry out these tasks in the order in which they are given, but as a check you could mark them off when you complete them. Add your own points to the list as soon as you think of them. (For 'Vicar' read priest, minister or incumbent of the church you have chosen.)

- ☐ Possible churches, date and time discussed
- ☐ Church(es) visited
- ☐ Firm arrangements made with Vicar
- ☐ Banns or licence applications made
- ☐ Reception venue, catering, music booked
- ☐ Wedding cake ordered
- ☐ Best man, attendants, ushers chosen and invited
- ☐ Guest list compiled
- ☐ Invitations bought or ordered
- ☐ Professional photographer/video maker booked and arrangement checked with church
- ☐ Present list compiled
- ☐ Notebook for recording presents started
- ☐ Honeymoon travel and accommodation booked
- ☐ Passports and visas obtained or renewed

- ☐ Form of service agreed with Vicar
- ☐ Hymns chosen
- ☐ Organist and choir booked
- ☐ Music for arrival and departure of bride and anthem agreed with Vicar and organist
- ☐ Arrangements for church bells discussed and agreed
- ☐ Buying and arranging of church flowers organised

- ☐ Wedding dress, head-dress and shoes bought
- ☐ Bridegroom's outfit bought or hire booked
- ☐ Best man and attendants outfits chosen/ordered
- ☐ Hairdressing appointments made

- ☐ Transport for bride and father, bridesmaids, bride's mother, bridegroom and best man arranged
- ☐ Travel from reception to airport/station/hotel arranged
- ☐ Cars booked and written confirmation received
- ☐ Transport arrangements made with guests (eg taking elderly carless guests to reception)
- ☐ Parking arrangements checked with church and explained to ushers and guests
- ☐ Bride's and attendants' bouquets organised

- [ ] Service sheet compiled and typed/produced on word processor ready for printer

---

- [ ] Wedding cakestand and knife organised
- [ ] Wedding ring(s) bought
- [ ] Service and duties explained to child attendants and best man
- [ ] Wedding service read over by both bride and bridegroom

- [ ] Date for wedding rehearsal(s) for couple alone and with attendants and parents fixed
- [ ] All church arrangements confirmed with Vicar
- [ ] Church seating planned and ushers informed
- [ ] Reception seating plan made and place cards produced
- [ ] Presents for attendants bought
- [ ] Numbers and menu checked with caterers
- [ ] Arrangements for flowers at reception checked
- [ ] Place for bride and groom to change after reception organised
- [ ] Return of any hired clothes arranged

- [ ] Wedding service read through again by bride and groom
- [ ] Final rehearsal attended
- [ ] Church and choir fees paid
- [ ] Banns Certificate or licence collected

- [ ] Honeymoon clothes and suitcases checked
- [ ] Written reminder or telephone call to check arrangements with car hire firm and photographer

---

- [ ] Final rehearsal
- [ ] Visit paid to church to see flowers
- [ ] Service read through again by bride and groom
- [ ] Entire wedding outfits tried on - before shops close
- [ ] Bride spends time alone thinking about her wedding
- [ ] Bride has a meal or spends time with her parents

The day has come at last!

If your marriage should encounter difficulties, it might improve the situation if you went to a service or spent a little time together in the church where you were married. If you felt that they would be able to help, you could ask to talk over the situation with the clergy.

Though the wedding service is over, clergy and congregations still care about couples who have been married in their church; they pray for them, take an interest in them, and share in thankfulness for the marriage.

The church, where a bride and groom make vows to each other and are pronounced to be Man and Wife, sees the beginning of a marriage which, with loyalty, self-giving and love, will give the couple companionship and delight for the rest of their lives. I hope you have a joyful wedding and that it will be the beginning of a long and happy life together.

Thank you certificates, published by Tim Tiley Ltd, are beautifully printed in blue and silver on an attractive textured card. They can be purchased in packs of 10 from Christian bookshops.